SCHOOL WORLD ATLAS

SCHOOL WORLD ATLAS

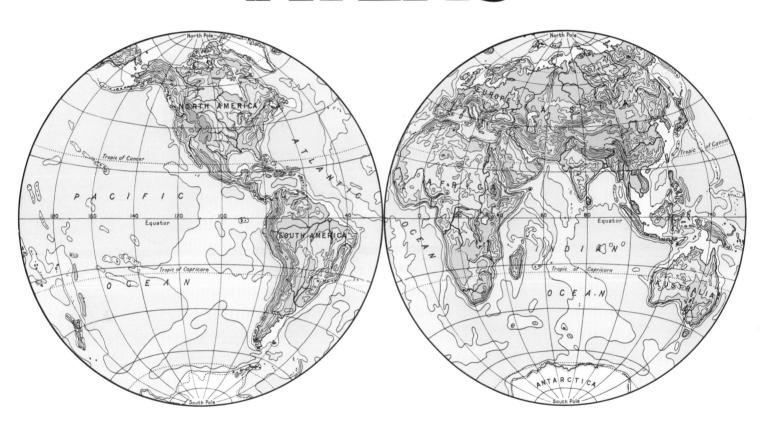

JOHN BARTHOLOMEW & SON LTD

Second Edition 1988

ISBN 0 7028 0764 8

Printed and Published in Scotland by
John Bartholomew & Son Ltd.
Edinburgh EH9 1TA.

A/B1053

CONTENTS

ENGLAND and WALES—PHYSICAL

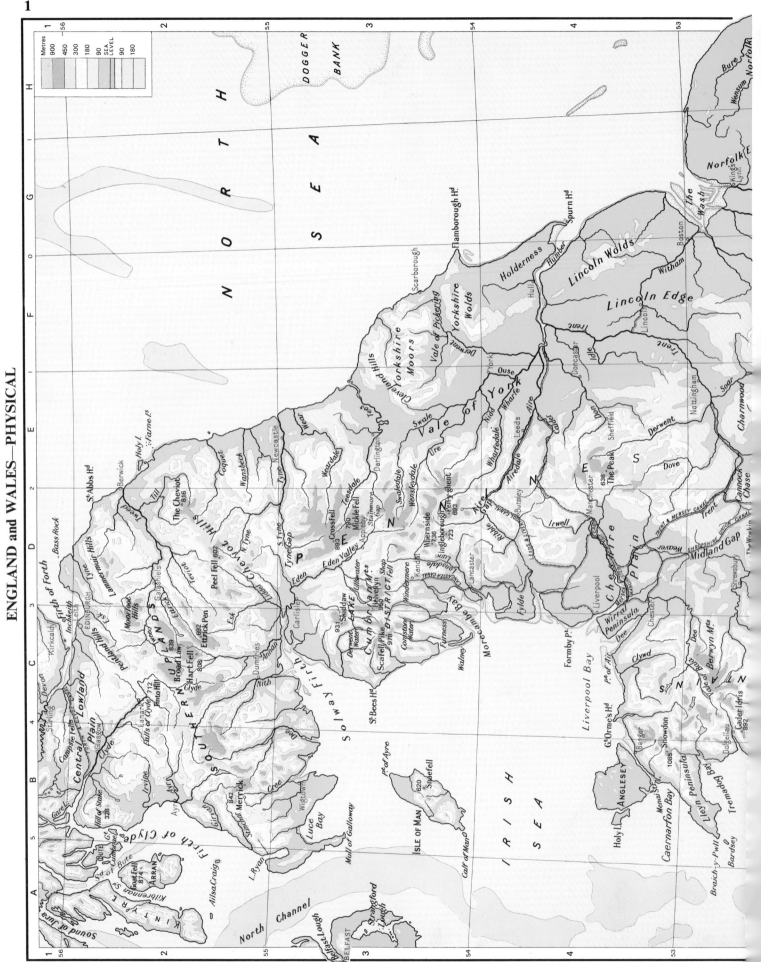

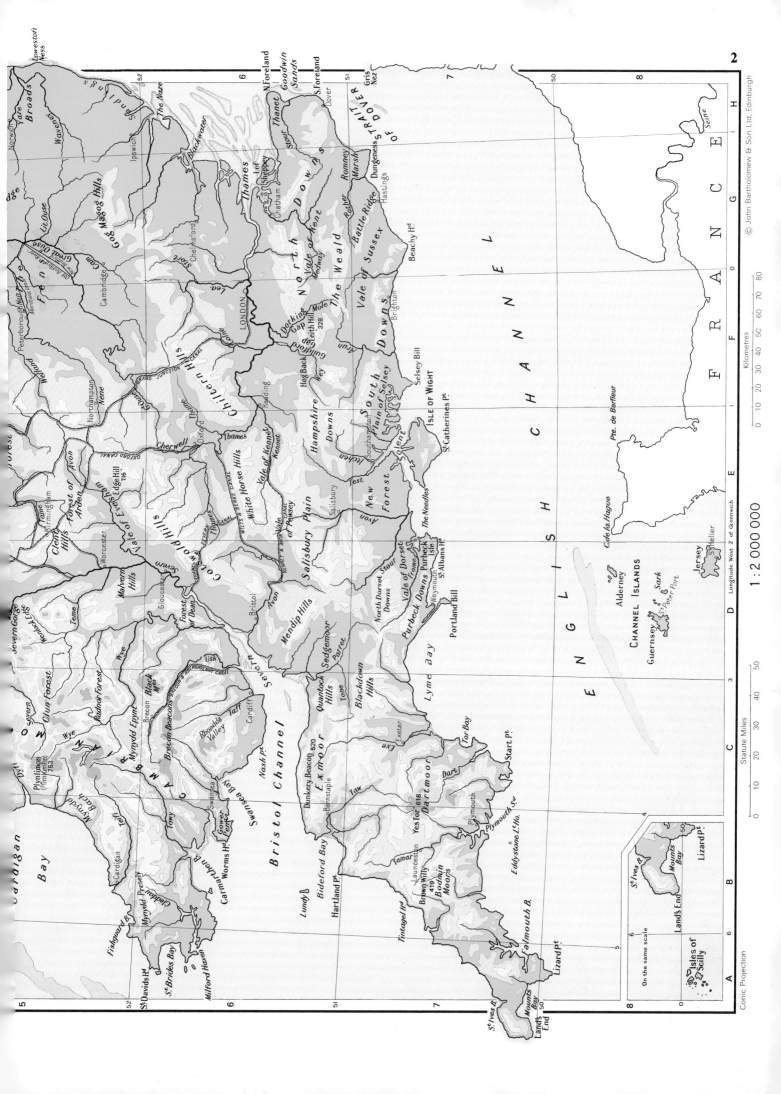

ENGLAND and WALES—POLITICAL

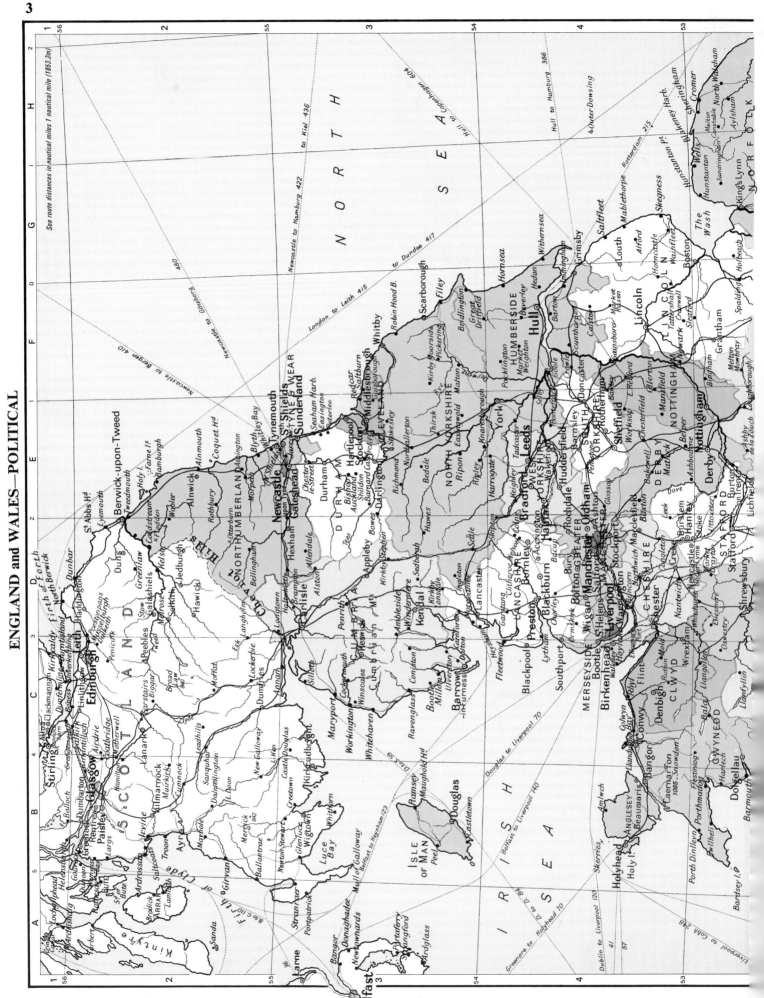

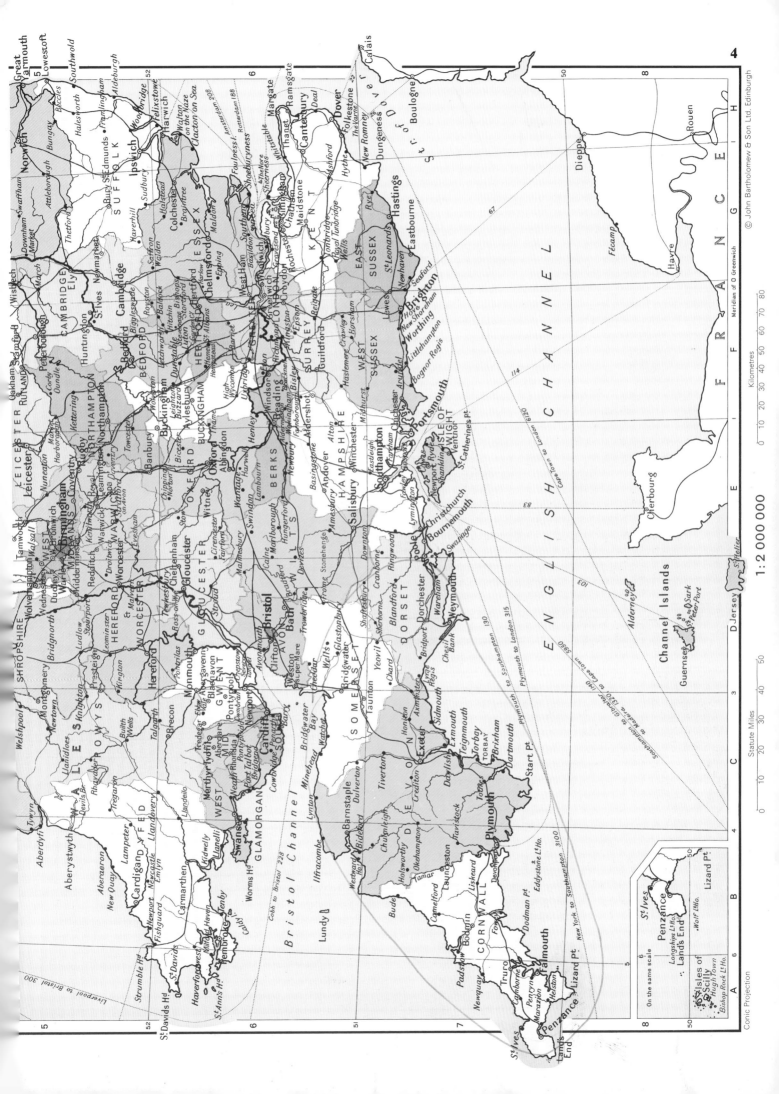

Metres
900
450
300
180
90
SEA LEVEL
90
180

SHETLAND ISLANDS

Unst
Yell
Fetlar
St Magnus Bay
Papa Stour
Whalsay
Lerwick
Bressay
Sumburgh Hd

ORKNEY ISLANDS

Westray
Papa Westray
Nth Ronaldsay
Rousay
Sanday
Shapinsay
Kirkwall
Scapa Flow
Burray
Hoy
Old Man of Hoy
Sth Ronaldsay
Pentland Firth
Dunnet Hd
Dunnet
Duncansby Hd
Thurso
Sinclairs B.
Noss Hd
Wick

N. Rona
Sula Sgier
Sule Skerry
Stack Skerry

Cape Wrath
L. Eriboll
Kyle of Tongue
Strathy Pt
Foinaven 908
Ben Hope 927
L. Loyal
Halladale
Thurso
Ben Hee 873
L. Naver
Ben Klibreck 961
Morven 705
Eddrachillis Bay
Las-Coul-Aulin Falls
Enard Bay
731
Ben More Assynt
Suilven 1027
Loch Shin
S. Oykel
Dornoch
Dornoch Firth
Tarbat Ness

Butt of Lewis
Flannan Is
LEWIS
Stornoway
North Minch
HARRIS
Scarp
Clisham 799
Taransay
Sound of Harris
Pabbay
Shiant Is
Gruinard B.
L. Broom
Falls of Measach
Ben Dearg 1087
Ben Wyvis 1045
Cromarty Firth
Moray Firth
Elgin
Banff
Kinnairds Head
Rattray Hd
Peterhead
Buchan Ness

N. Uist
Benbecula
Little Minch
L. Snizort
S. of Raasay
Raasay
Rona
Gair Loch
Loch Torridon
L. Maree
Slioch 994
L. Fannich
L. Monar
Black Isle
Culbin Forest
Spey
Deveron
Ythan
Don

SKYE
Cuillin Hills
L. Alsh
Falls of Glomach
L. Mullardoch
Mam Soul 1031
Meall Fuarvounie 696
Beauly
Inverness
Ness
Nairn
Findhorn
Carn Mor 803
Morven 872
Hill of Fare 471
Girdle Ness
Aberdeen
Dee

Ben More S. Uist 620
Cuillin
L. Scavaig
Ben Attow
Glen Moriston
Falls of Foyers
Monadhliath Mts
Cairngorms
Cairn Toul 1293
Ben Macdui 1309
Braemar
Lochnagar 1154
Glas Maol 1067
N. Esk
Mearns

Barra
Oigh-sgeir
Canna
Rum
Eigg
Muck
Sound of Sleat
L. Morar
L. Shiel
Hourn
Glen Garry
L. Oich
Corrieyairack
L. Arkaig
L. Lochy
L. Laggan
Drumochter Pass
Ben Dearg 1007
Ben-y-Gloe 1119
Glen Garry
Battock 779
N. Esk
Montrose

Barra Hd
Coll
Ardnamurchan Pt
Morvern
L. Sunart
L. Eil
Fort William
Ben Nevis 1344
Ben Alder 1145
L. Ericht
L. Rannoch
Tummel
Schiehallion 1081
Pass of Killiecrankie
Isla
S. Esk

Tiree
Staffa
Iona
Mull
Ben More 966
L. Linnhe
L. Etive
Glen Coe
Rannoch Moor
Ben Lawers 1214
L. Tay
Tay
Strathmore
Sidlaw Hills
Dundee
Buddon Ness
Bell Rock

Skerryvore
Dubh Artach
Colonsay
Str. of Corryvreckan
Oban
Ben Cruachan 1124
Ben Lui 1130
Ben More 1171
L. Earn
Ben Vorlich 983
Loch Awe
Larn
Almond
Perth
Carse of Gowrie
Firth of Tay
Ochil Hills
Howe of Fife Eden
Lomond Hills
Fife Ness
L. of May

Sound of Jura
L. Katrine
Trossachs
Ben Lomond 973
Forth
Teith
L. Leven
Kirkcaldy
Bass Rock
Inchkeith
Leith

JURA
Raps of Jura 784
Firth of Lorn
Loch Fyne
L. Lomond
Garel
Stirling
Devon
Firth of Forth

ISLAY
Bute
Cumbrae
Hill of Stake 522
Central Lowlands
Glasgow
Clyde
EDINBURGH
Tyne
Esk
St Abb's Hd
Campsie Fells
Forth & Clyde Canal
Pentland Hills
Lammermuir Hills
Berwick

Mull of Oa
Gigha
Sd of Bute
Goat Fell 874
ARRAN
Irvine
Lanark
Falls of Clyde
Moorfoot Hills
The Merse
Tweed
Holy I.
Farne Is

Inishtrahull
Kilbrennan Sd
Firth of Clyde
Ayr
Tinto Hill 712
Culter Fell 748
Broad Law 839
St Mary's L.
Ettrick
Galashiels
Tweed
SOUTHERN UPLANDS
Teviotdale
The Cheviot 816
Coquet

Rathlin I.
Mull of Kintyre
Fair Hd
Ailsa Craig
Girvan
Tweedsmuir Hills
Hart Fell 808
Ettrick Pen 692
Teviot
Hawick
Peel Fell 602
Wansbeck
N. Tyne

Giant's Causeway
North Channel
Lead Hills 796
Lowther 732
Annandale
Liddesdale
Liddel
Cheviot Hills

Inishowen
Sperrin Mts
Sawel Mt
Lough Foyle
Coleraine
Plateau of Antrim
554 Trostan
Garron Pt
Bann
Derry

Merrick 842
Hells Range
Carsphairn
Cairnsmore
L. Doon
Nithsdale
Dumfries
Esk
Carlisle
Eden
Tyne Gap
S. Tyne
Newcastle

Galloway
L. Ryan
Gl. App
Stinchar
L. Ken
Nith
Annan
Criffell 569
Tyne

Wigtown
Luce Bay
Mull of Galloway

WESTERN HIGHLANDS
The Great Glen or Glen More
GRAMPIAN MOUNTAINS
OUTER HEBRIDES
INNER HEBRIDES
ATLANTIC OCEAN
NORTH SEA

Conic Projection

Statute Miles
0　10　20　30　40

1 : 2 000 000

Kilometres
0　10　20　30　40　50　60　70

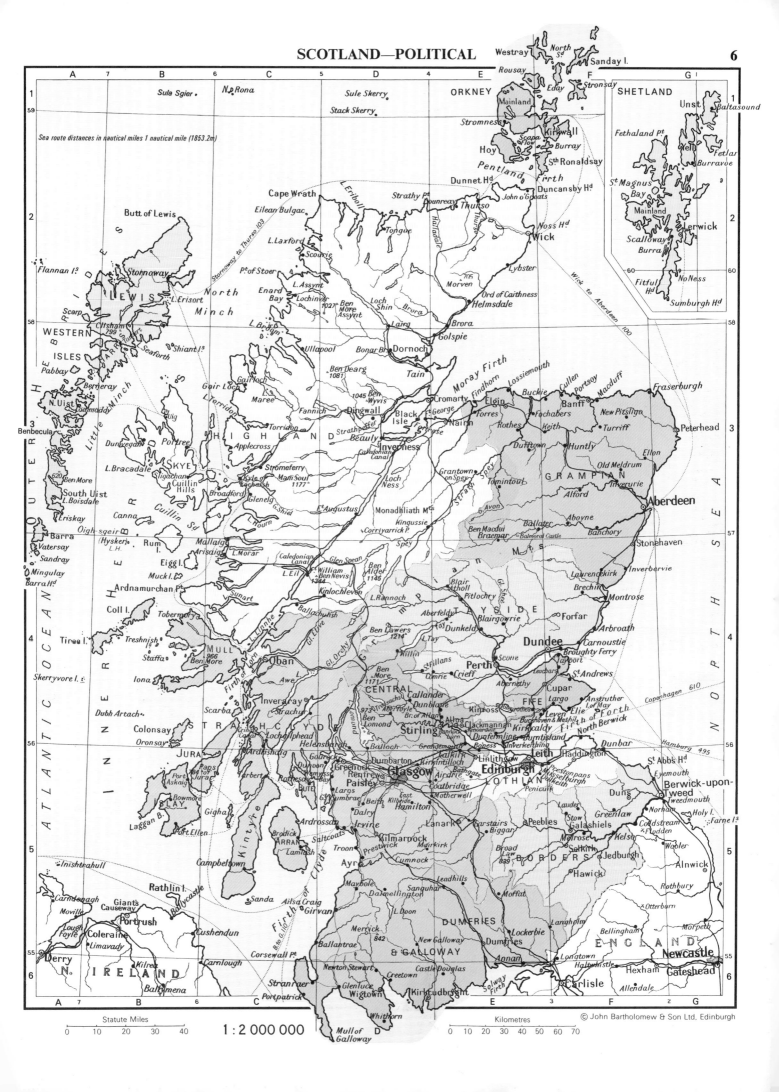

Scale 1 : 2 000 000

Statute Miles
0 10 20 30 40

Kilometres
0 10 20 30 40 50 60 70

© John Bartholomew & Son Ltd, Edinburgh

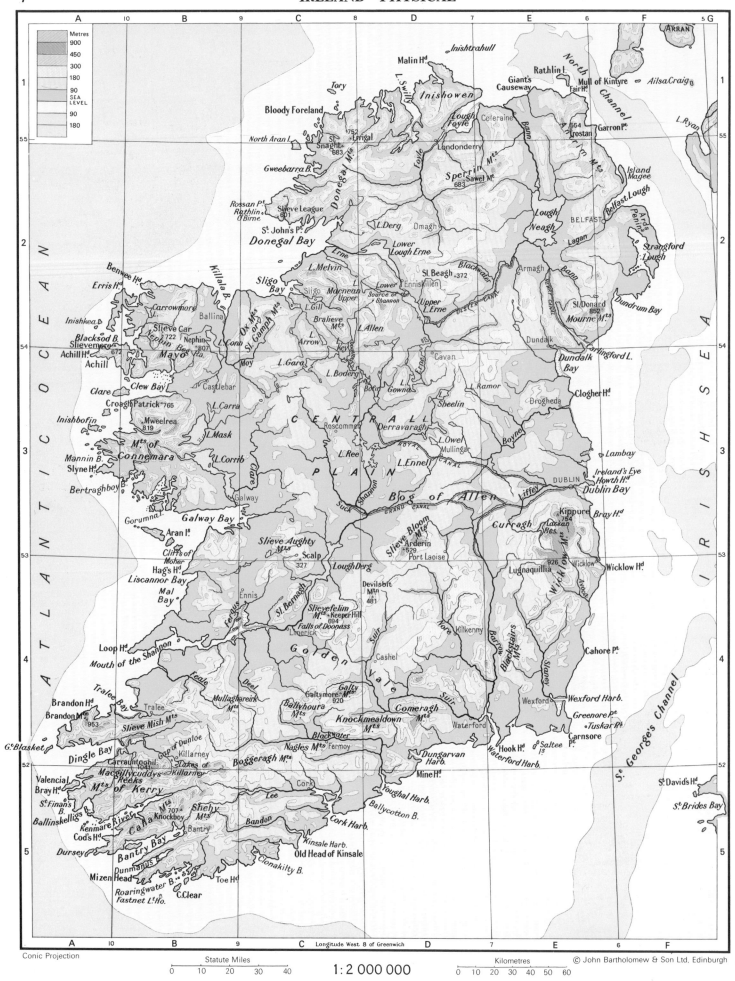

Conic Projection

Statute Miles

0   10   20   30   40

1 : 2 000 000

Kilometres

0   10   20   30   40   50   60

© John Bartholomew & Son Ltd, Edinburgh

Longitude West 8 of Greenwich

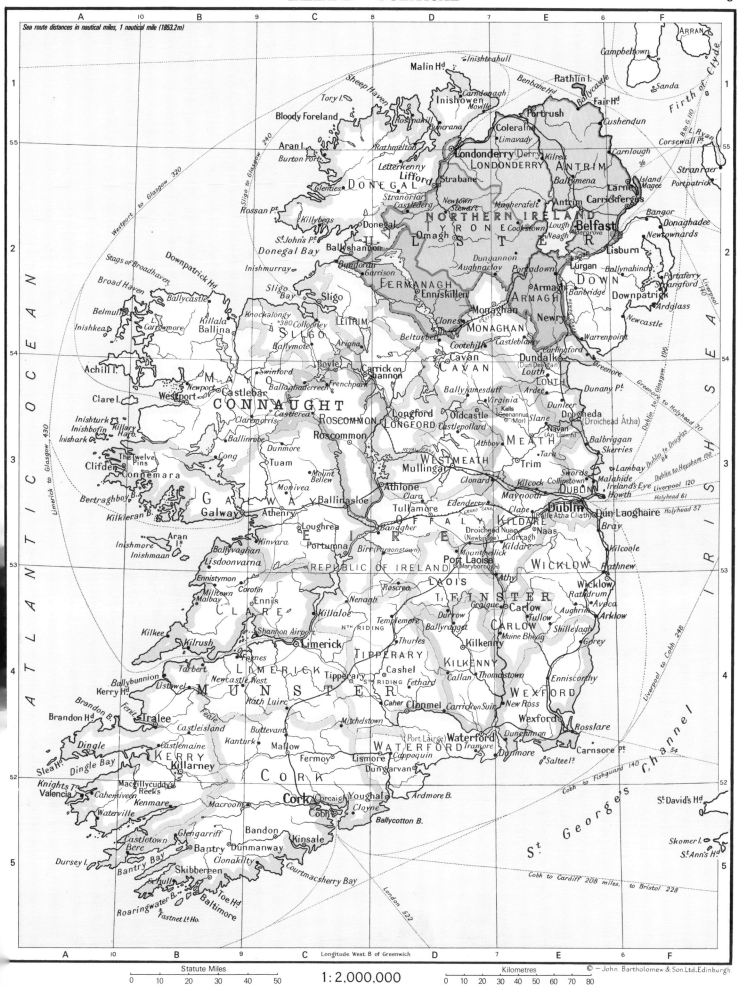

Sea route distances in nautical miles, 1 nautical mile (1853.2m)

ARRAN

Firth of Clyde

Campbeltown

Sanda

Inishtrahull

Malin Hd

Benbane Hd

Rathlin I.

Ballycastle

Fair Hd

Cushendun

L. Ryan

Corsewall Pt

Carndonagh
Moville

Portrush

Inishowen

Coleraine

Limavady

Kilrea

Carnlough

Stranraer

Island Magee

Portpatrick

Sheep Haven

Tory I.

Bloody Foreland

Rosnakill

Buncrana

Londonderry Derry

LONDONDERRY

ANTRIM

Ballymena

Larne

Carrickfergus

Aran I.

Rathmelton

Letterkenny

Strabane

Newtown Stewart

Magherafelt

Antrim

Lough Neagh

Bangor

Donaghadee

Newtownards

Burton Port

Lifford

Glenties

DONEGAL

Cookstown

Belfast

Rossan Pt.

Stranorlar
Castlederg

NORTHERN IRELAND

Moira

Lisburn

Killybegs

Donegal

TYRONE

Omagh

U L S T E R

Dungannon

Portadown

Lagan

Lurgan

Ballynahinch

St. John's Pt.

Ballyshannon

Aughnacloy

Armagh

DOWN

Downpatrick

Stags of Broadhaven

Downpatrick Hd

FERMANAGH

Enniskillen

ARMAGH

Banbridge

Ardglass

Inishmurray

Bundoran
Garrison

Monaghan

Newry

Newcastle

Broad Haven

Sligo Bay

Clones

MONAGHAN

Warrenpoint

Belmullet

Ballycastle

Sligo

Belturbet

Cootehill

Carlingford

Greenore

Dundalk

Inishkea

Killala
Carrowmore

Knockalongy

LEITRIM

Castleblaney

(Dun Dealgan)

Greenore to Holyhead 70

Achill I.

Ballina

Collooney

380

Cavan

CAVAN

Louth

LOUTH

Dunany Pt

Arigna

Ballymote

Ballyjamesduff

Ardee

Dunleer

Clare I.

MAYO

Swinford

Boyle

Carrick on Shannon

Virginia

Kells
Ceanannus Mor

Slane

Droichead

Drogheda

(Droichead Átha)

Newport

Castlebar

Ballaghaderreen

Frenchpark

Longford

Oldcastle

Navan
(An Uaimh)

Balbriggan

Westport

CONNAUGHT

Clonmances

Castlerea

ROSCOMMON

LONGFORD

Castlepollard

MEATH

Swords

Skerries

Ballinrobe

Roscommon

Athboy

Tara

Lambay I.

The Twelve Pins

Cong

Dunmore

WESTMEATH

Trim

Malahide

Inishturk

Killary Harb.

Clifden

Monivea

Mount Bellew

Mullingar

Clonard

Kilcock

Collinstown

Ireland's Eye

Howth

Inishbofin

Tuam

Athlone

Maynooth

DUBLIN

Inishark

Connemara

GALWAY

Ballinasloe

Clara

Edenderry

Clane

Holyhead 61

Bertraghboy B.

Athenry

Tullamore

OFFALY

KILDARE

Dublin

Dún Laoghaire

Holyhead 57

Galway

Loughrea

Bandgher

Baile Átha Cliath

Kilkieran B.

Portumna

EIRE

Birr (Parsonstown)

Naas

Bray

Aran Is.

Kinvara

Mountmellick

Kildare

Kilcoole

Inishmore

Inishmaan

Ballyvaghan

Droichead Nua
(Newbridge)

Curragh

Lisdoonvarna

REPUBLIC OF IRELAND

Port Laoise

WICKLOW

Rathnew

Ennistymon

(Maryborough)

Roscrea

LAOIS

Athy

Wicklow

Corofin

LEINSTER

Rathdrum

Milltown Malbay

Ennis

Nenagh

Templemore

Durrow

Graigue

Carlow

Aughrim

Avoca

Arklow

CLARE

Killaloe

CARLOW

Tullow

Shillelagh

Kilkee

Shannon Airport

Thurles

Ballyragget

Muine Bheag

Gorey

Kilrush

TIPPERARY

Cashel

Kilkenny

Limerick

Faynes

NTH. RIDING

KILKENNY

Enniscorthy

Tarbert

Tipperary

STH. RIDING

Fethard

Callan

Thomastown

WEXFORD

Ballybunnion

LIMERICK

Caher

Clonmel

Carrick on Suir

New Ross

Kerry Hd

Listowel

Newcastle West

MUNSTER

Mitchelstown

Wexford

Brandon B.

Fenit

Feale

Rath Luirc

Waterford

Duncannon

Brandon Hd

Tralee

Castleisland

Buttevant

Kanturk

Mallow

Lismore

Cappoquin

(Port Láirge)

Tramore

Rosslare

Dingle

Castlemaine

WATERFORD

Dungarvan

Dunmore

Carnsore Pt

Slea Hd

Killarney

Fermoy

CORK

Saltee Is.

Dingle Bay

KERRY

Macroom

Youghal

Ardmore B.

St George's Channel

Knights Tn

MacGillycuddy's Reeks

Cork

Corcaigh

Cloyne

St David's Hd

Valencia

Cahersiveen

Kenmare

Cobh

Ballycotton B.

Waterville

Glengarriff

Bandon

Kinsale

Skomer I.

Castletown Bere

Bantry

Dunmanway

Clonakilty

St Ann's Hd

Dursey I.

Bantry Bay

Skibbereen

Schull

Toe Hd

Baltimore

Roaringwater B.

Fastnet Lt. Ho.

Cobh to Cardiff 208 miles, to Bristol 228

Statute Miles

0 10 20 30 40 50

1:2,000,000

Kilometres

0 10 20 30 40 50 60 70 80

© — John Bartholomew & Son Ltd. Edinburgh

Longitude West 8 of Greenwich

Lambert's Zenithal Equal Area Projection

Longitude East 10 of Greenwich

© John Bartholomew & Son Ltd, Edinburgh

N.B. While the Ural Mountains form the traditional boundary of Europe, it is more convenient to treat U.S.S.R. as in Eurasia.

Statute Miles
0 100 200 300 400

Kilometres
0 100 200 300 400 500 600

1:18 000 000

N.B. While the Ural Mountains form the traditional boundary of Europe, it is more convenient to treat U.S.S.R. as in Eurasia.

Sea route distances in nautical miles
1 nautical mile (1853.2m)

Lambert's Zenithal Equal Area Projection

Statute Miles

0   100   200   300   400

Kilometres

0   100   200   300   400   500   600

1 : 18 000 000

© John Bartholomew & Son Ltd, Edinburgh

Longitude East 10 of Greenwich

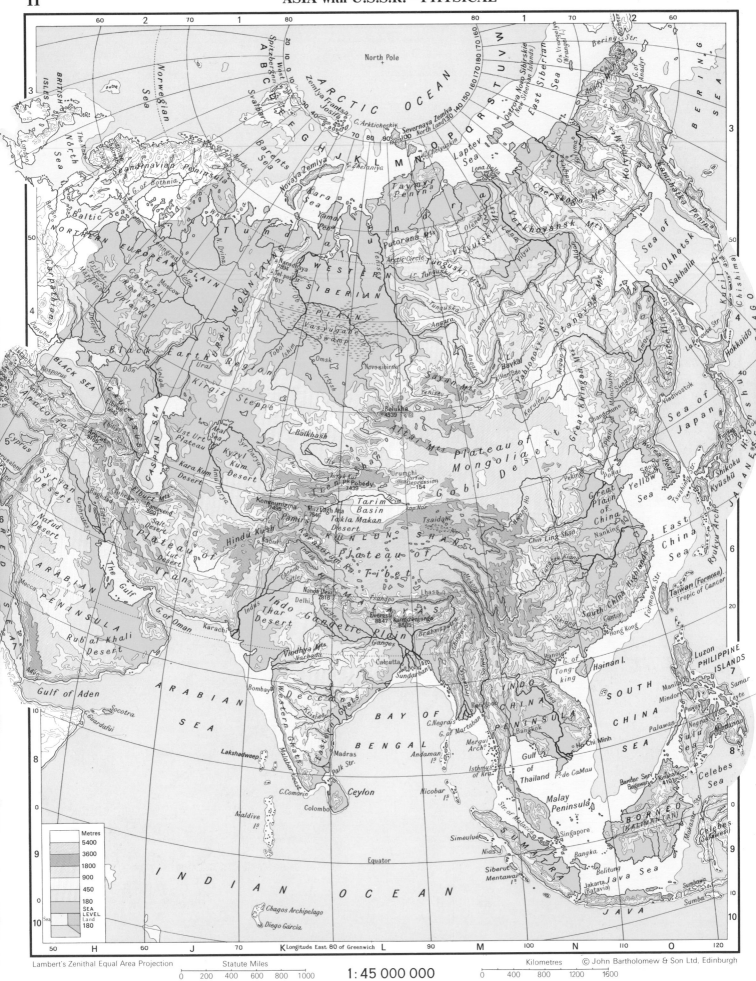

Lambert's Zenithal Equal Area Projection

Statute Miles

1 : 45 000 000

Kilometres

© John Bartholomew & Son Ltd, Edinburgh

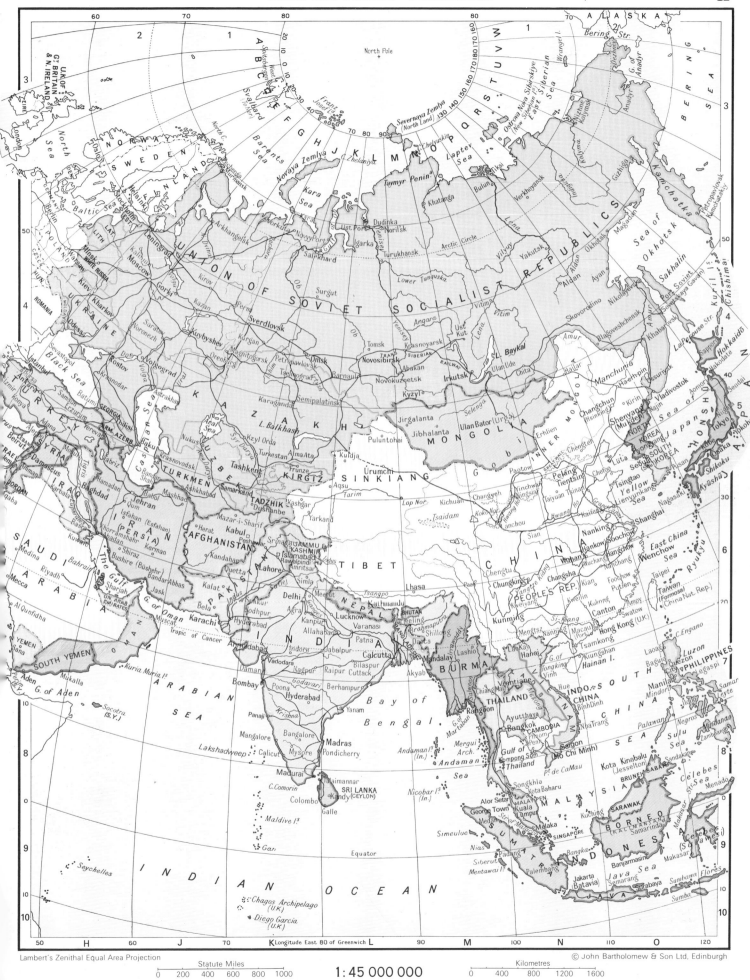

Lambert's Zenithal Equal Area Projection

© John Bartholomew & Son Ltd, Edinburgh

Statute Miles
0   200   400   600   800   1000

Kilometres
0   400   800   1200   1600

1 : 45 000 000

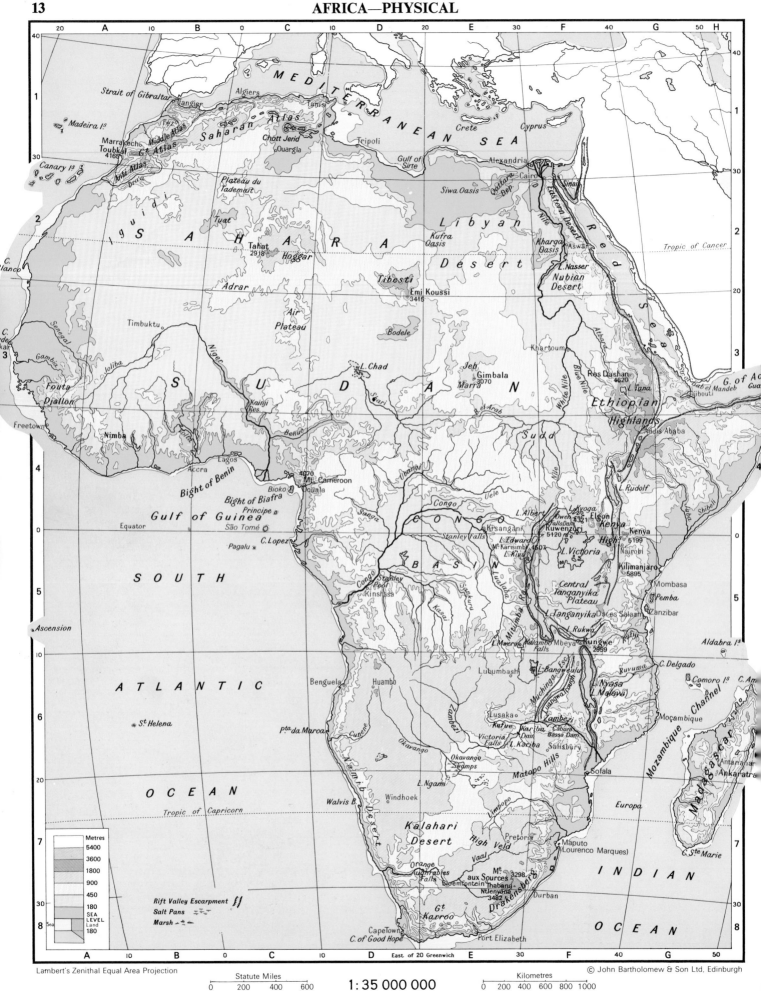

Lambert's Zenithal Equal Area Projection

Statute Miles
0   200   400   600

1 : 35 000 000

Kilometres
0   200   400   600   800   1000

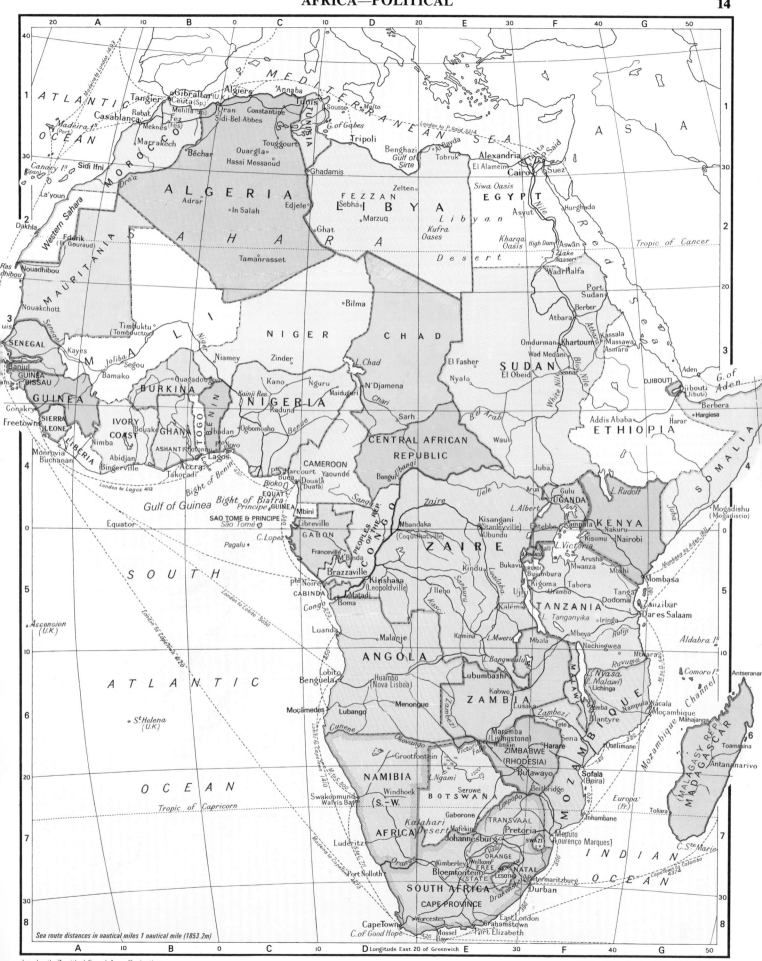

Lambert's Zenithal Equal Area Projection

Statute Miles

0 200 400 600

1:35 000 000

Kilometres

0 200 400 600 800 1000

Sea route distances in nautical miles 1 nautical mile (1853.2m)

© John Bartholomew & Son Ltd, Edinburgh

Lambert's Zenithal Equal Area Projection

Statute Miles
0   200   400   600

Longitude West 100 of Greenwich

Kilometres
0   200   400   600   800   1000

1 : 30 000 000

© John Bartholomew
& Son Ltd, Edinburgh

Metres
5400
3600
1800
900
450
180
SEA LEVEL
Land
180
Sea

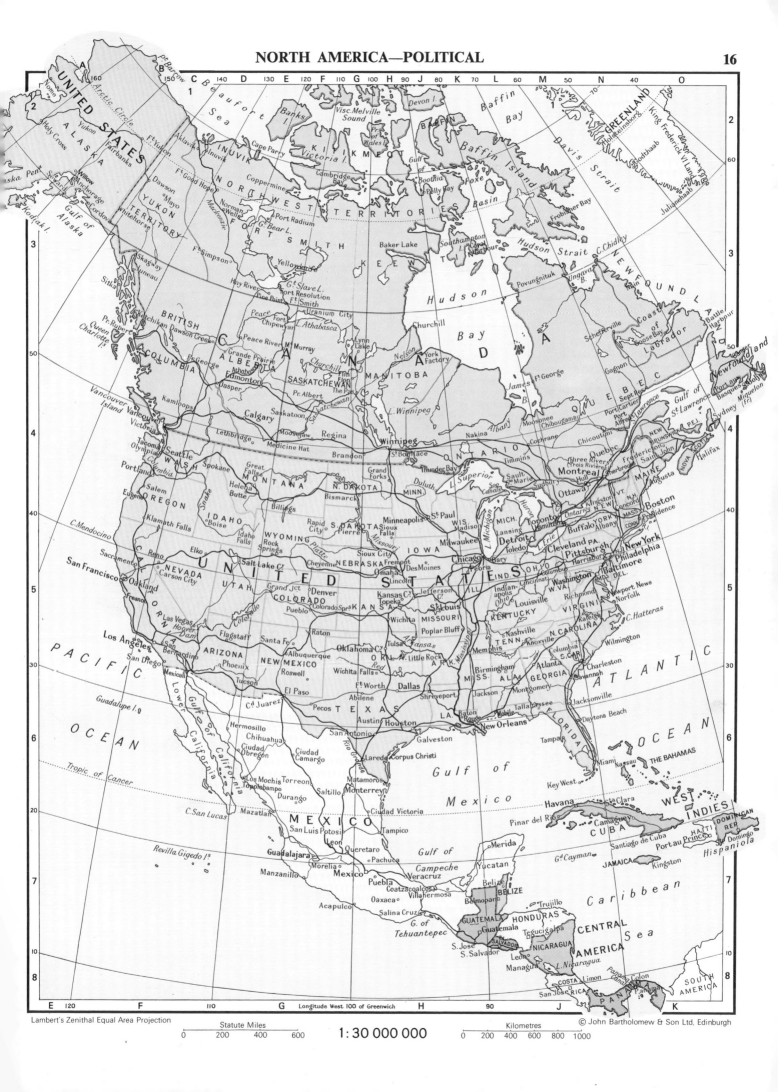

Lambert's Zenithal Equal Area Projection

Statute Miles

0   200   400   600

1 : 30 000 000

Kilometres

0   200   400   600   800   1000

© John Bartholomew & Son Ltd, Edinburgh

Lambert's Zenithal Equal Area Projection

© John Bartholomew & Son Ltd., Edinburgh

Statute Miles

0   200   400   600

Kilometres

0   200   400   600   800   1000

1 : 30 000 000

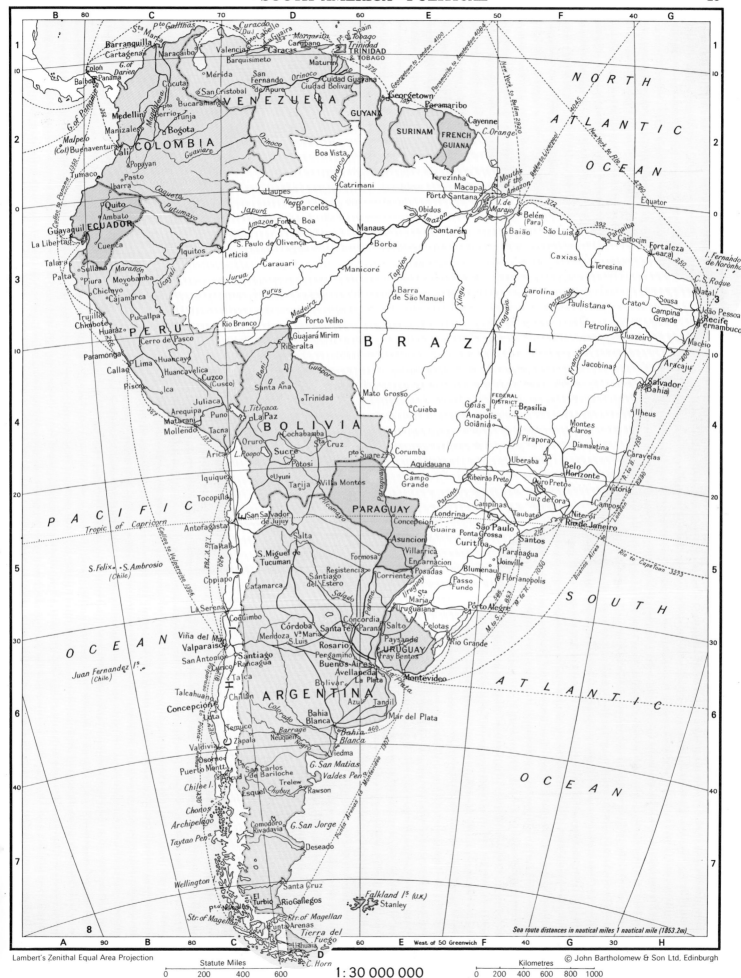

Lambert's Zenithal Equal Area Projection

Statute Miles

0   200   400   600

Kilometres

0   200   400   600   800   1000

1 : 30 000 000

© John Bartholomew & Son Ltd, Edinburgh

Sea route distances in nautical miles 1 nautical mile (1853.2m)

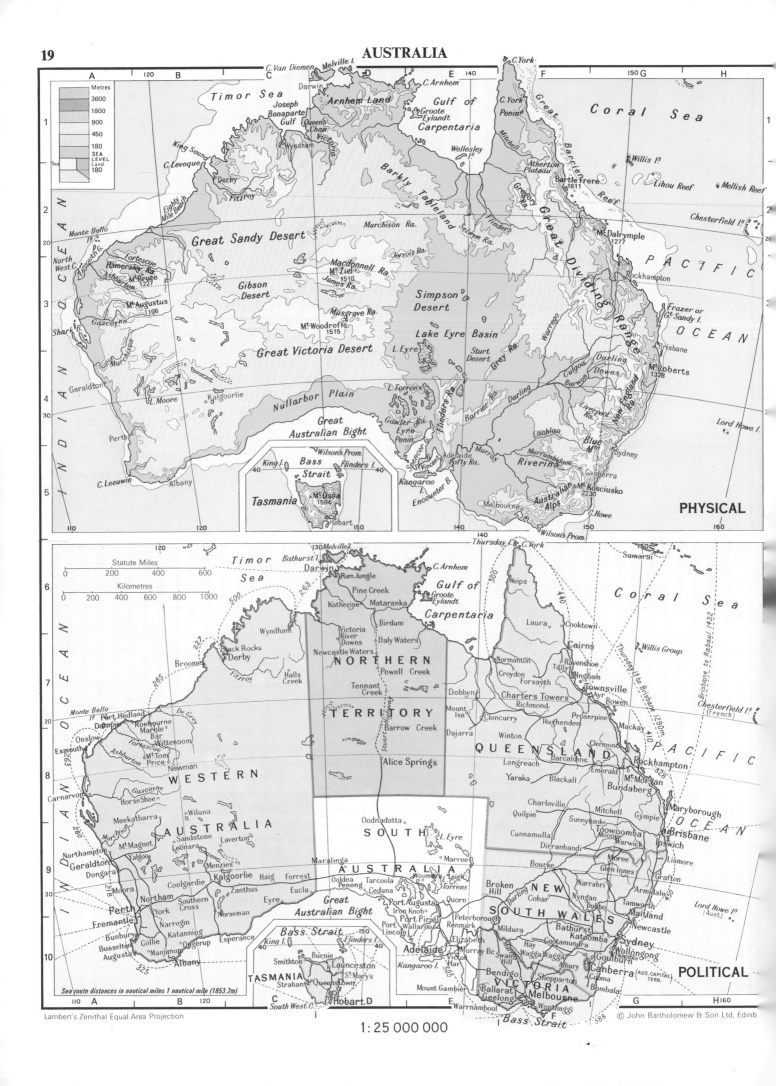

PHYSICAL

POLITICAL

Lambert's Zenithal Equal Area Projection

1 : 25 000 000

© John Bartholomew & Son Ltd, Edinb

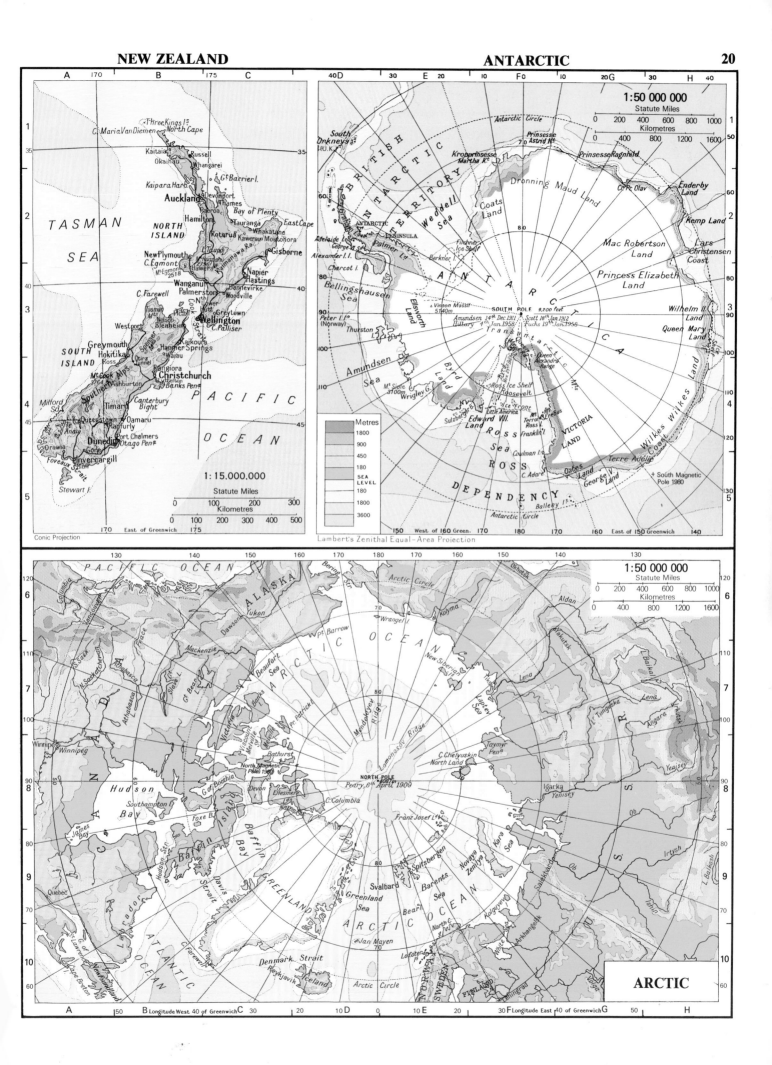

NEW ZEALAND

Three Kings Is.
C. Maria Van Diemen   North Cape
Kaitaia   Russell
Okaihau   Whangarei
Kaipara Harb.   Gt. Barrier I.
Devonport
Auckland   Thames
Paeroa   Bay of Plenty
Hamilton   Tauranga
NORTH   Rotorua   Whakatane
ISLAND   Kawerau Moutohora   East Cape
Gisborne
New Plymouth   L. Taupo
C. Egmont   Mt Ruapehu
Mt Egmont   2797
2518   Hawera   Napier
Wanganui   Hastings
C. Farewell   Palmerston   Dannevirke
Nth.   Woodville
Tasman   Lower
Mts.   Nelson   Greytown
Takaka   **Wellington**
Westport   Blenheim   C. Palliser
SOUTH   Kaikoura
ISLAND   Greymouth   Hanmer Springs
Hokitika   Wairau
Ross   Rangiora
Mt Cook Nps.   Christchurch
3764   Ashburton   Banks Pen.
Milford   Southern Alps
Sd.   Timaru
Te   Queenstown   Oamaru
Anau   Ranfurly
Orawia   Gore   Dunedin
Foveaux Strait   Invercargill
Stewart I.

TASMAN
SEA

PACIFIC
OCEAN

1:15,000,000

Statute Miles
0   100   200   300
Kilometres
0   100   200   300   400   500

Conic Projection
East of Greenwich

ANTARCTIC

1:50 000 000

Statute Miles
0   200   400   600   800   1000
Kilometres
0   400   800   1200   1600

Antarctic Circle
South Orkneys (U.K.)
Prinsesse Astrid Kt.
Kronprinsesse Martha Kt.
Prinsesse Ragnhild
BRITISH ANTARCTIC TERRITORY
Dronning Maud Land
C. R. Olav
Enderby Land
Weddell Sea
Coats Land
Kemp Land
ANTARCTIC PENINSULA
Adelaide I.
George VI Sd.
Palmer Ld.
Filchner Ice Shelf
Mac Robertson Land
Lars Christensen Coast
Alexander I. I.
Berkner I.
Princess Elizabeth Land
Charcot I.
Bellingshausen Sea
Vinson Massif 5140m
SOUTH POLE 9,200 feet
Wilhelm II Land
Peter I I.
Ellsworth Land
Amundsen 14th Dec 1911.   Scott 18th Jan 1912
Hillary 4th Jan 1958.   Fuchs 19th Jan 1958
Queen Mary Land
Thurston I.
ANTARCTICA
Trans antarctic
Amundsen Sea
Byrd Land
Queen Alexandra Range
Mt Siple 3100m
Wrigley G.
Ross Ice Shelf
Roosevelt
Sulzberger
Edward VII Land
Little America
Ice Front
Mt Terror
Mt Erebus
Ross Sea
Franklin I.
VICTORIA LAND
Wilkes Land
DEPENDENCY
Coulman I.
Terre Adélie
C. Adare
Oates Land
George V Land
+ South Magnetic Pole 1980
Balleny Is.
Antarctic Circle
West of 160 Green.
East of 150 Greenwich

Metres	
	1800
	900
	450
	180
SEA LEVEL	
	180
	1800
	3600

Lambert's Zenithal Equal-Area Projection

ARCTIC

PACIFIC OCEAN
ALASKA
Columbia
Vancouver I.
Yukon
Bering Str.
Arctic Circle
Okhotsk
Aldan
Dawson
Pt. Barrow
Wrangel I.
Kolyma
Mackenzie
Beaufort Sea
New Siberian Is.
Lena
Gt. Slave L.
Banks I.
ARCTIC OCEAN
Yakutsk
Lena
Saskatchewan
Athabasca
Victoria I.
Pr. Patrick I.
Melville I.
Mendeleyev Ridge
Laptev Sea
L. Baikal
Viscount Melville Sd.
Bathurst
Lomonosov Ridge
C. Chelyuskin
North Land
Angara
Yenisey
Winnipeg
North Magnetic Pole 1980
G. of Boothia
Devon
NORTH POLE 4087m
Peary, 6th April 1909
Taymyr Pen.
L. Tunguska
Hudson Bay
Southampton I.
Ellesmere
Nares Str.
C. Columbia
Igarka
Yenisey
U. S. S. R.
Irtysh
James Bay
Foxe Chan.
Baffin Island
Baffin Bay
Franz Josef Ld.
Ob
Quebec
Labrador
Hudson Str.
Davis Strait
Spitsbergen
Novaya Zemlya
Kara Sea
Salekhard
Ob
GREENLAND
Barents Sea
Irtysh
G. of St. Lawrence
Cape Breton
C. Farewell
Greenland Sea
Bear I.
North C.
Kolguyev I.
Newfoundland
ATLANTIC OCEAN
Denmark Strait
Jan Mayen
ARCTIC OCEAN
Arkhangelsk
Volga
Quebec
Reykjavik
Iceland
Lofoten Is.
NORWAY SWEDEN FINLAND
Leningrad
Denmark Strait
Arctic Circle
Longitude West of Greenwich
Longitude East of Greenwich

1:50 000 000

Statute Miles
0   200   400   600   800   1000
Kilometres
0   400   800   1200   1600

ARCTIC

TIME WHEN NOON AT GREENWICH MIDNIGHT

V VI VII VIII IX X XI P.M. XII I A.M. II III IV V

ARCTIC OCEAN

Laptev Sea

East Siberian Sea

Beaufort Sea

Taymyr Peninsula

U.S.A

UNION of SOVIET SOCIALIST REPUBLICS

ALASKA

YUKON TERRITORY

NORTHWEST TERRITORIES

MACKENZIE DISTRICT

Sea of Okhotsk

Bering Sea

Gulf of Alaska

BRITISH COLUMBIA

CAN

A S I A

MONGOLIA

Sea of Japan

Vancouver I.

NORTH

ALBERTA SASKATCHEWAN

Gobi

INNER MONGOL

Vancouver Seattle

Portland

UNITED

CHINA (PEOPLES REP.)

Tokyo
Yokohama

Salt Lake City

San Francisco

TIBET

Shanghai

Yokohama to Vancouver 4344

Yokohama to San Francisco 4536

Los Angeles

INDIA

Hong Kong

Yokohama to Honolulu 3380

Midway Is. (U.S.)

Honolulu to Vancouver 2430 m.

Honolulu to S.F. 2100

Tropic of Cancer

Honolulu to L.A. 2228

MEXICO

Bombay
Madras

Bay of Bengal

THAILAND

Hainan

China Sea

Luzon
Manila
Quezon City
PHILIPPINES

Marianas

Saipan I.

Wake I. (U.S.)

Guam (U.S.) Honolulu 3337
Johnston I. (U.S.)

Honolulu Hawaii (U.S.)
Pearl Har.

Honolulu to Panama 4710

Mexico

SRI LANKA
Colombo

Saigon (Ho Chi Minh)

Mindanao

Caroline Is.
Palau

Bikini
Marshall Is.

P A C I F I C O C E A N

Palmyra I. (U.S.)
Washington I. Fanning I.
Christmas I.

EAST INDIES
Singapore Borneo

Halmahera

Equator

Nauru Banaba

Phoenix Is.

Jarvis I. Malden I.
Starbuck I.

Equator

Sumatra
Jakarta Batavia
Java

Sulawesi

Moluccas New Guinea

Solomon Is.

Tuvalu

Tokelau Is.

Caroline I. (Fr.)

Marquesas Is. (Fr.)

Auckland to Panama 6590

INDIAN

Timor Darwin

Torres Str.
Coral Sea

P. Moresby

Vanuatu
(New Hebrides)

St. Cruz

Rotuma
Fiji
Suva

Samoa
Tutuila (U.S.)

Tongareva (Penrhyn)
Suvorov I. Manihiki Is.

Rakahanga

Society Is. (Fr.)
Cook Is. Tahiti

Tuamotu Archipelago (Fr.)

OCEAN

Tropic of Capricorn

NORTHERN TERRITORY
QUEENSLAND

Townsville

Rockhampton Noumea New Caledonia (Fr.)

Tubuai Is.
(Austral Is.)

Tropic of Capricorn

Pitcairn I.

Ducie I.

Easter I.
(Chile)

WESTERN AUSTRALIA

AUSTRALIA

Alice Springs

Brisbane

Norfolk I.

Durban to Fremantle 4248
Durban to Adelaide 5100

SOUTH AUSTRALIA

Geraldton
Perth

NEW SOUTH WALES
Newcastle

Darling

Lord Howe I.

Kermadec Is.

Amsterdam I. (Fr)

Fremantle

Great Australian Bight

Adelaide

Canberra Sydney

Auckland

CapeTown to Adelaide 5600
CapeTown to Hobart 5840

VICTORIA
Melbourne

Tasman Sea

NEW ZEALAND
Wellington

Wellington to Rio de Janeiro 6980

Tasmania Hobart

Christchurch
Dunedin

Stewart I.

Chatham Is.

Bounty Is.
Antipodes
Auckland I.

Heard I.

Campbell I.

Macquarie I.

Principal Shipping Routes according to traffic
Distances given in Nautical Miles : One Nautical Mile (1853.2m)

Seas open to Navigation the whole year

Principal Railways

Air Routes

Kaiser Wilhelm II Land
Queen Mary Land

Wilkes Land

A 90 B 120 C 150 D 180 E 150 F 120 G

SVALBARD
West Spitsbergen
Edge I.
South C.
Queen
Louise Ld
C. Bismarck
Ingefield Ld
Prudhoe Ld
Hayes
Peninsula
Melville
B.
GREENLAND
King
William Ld
King
Christian IX
Land
Scoresby L.
Scoresbysund
Baffin
Bay
Upernavik
Jan Mayen
B a r e n t s
S e a
Novaya Zemlya
Kara
Sea
Taymyr Pen
Taymyr
North Cape
Bear I.
Tromsö
Lofoten Is
Arctic Circle
Murmansk
Yamal
Penin
Khal'mer Yu
Novy Port
Igarka
Yenisey
Lower Tunguska

UNION of SOVIET
SOCIALIST REPUBLICS

A S I A

MONGOLIA
Gobi
CHINA
TIBET
Lhasa

ATLANTIC
OCEAN

AFRICA

INDIAN OCEAN

SOUTH AMERICA

BRAZIL

ARGENTINA

Falkland Is

C. Horn
Drake Str.

South Georgia
South
Sandwich
Group

Bouvet I.
(Nor.)

Pr. Edward I.
Marion I.
Crozet Is
(Fr.)

Kerguelen I (Fr)

Heard I.

South Shetlands
South Orkneys
Graham Ld
Adelaide I.

Antarctic Circle
Enderby Ld
Kemp Ld
Kaiser
Wilhelm II
Land
Queen Mary
Land

INDEX

This is a selected index, naming principal administrative divisions as scale permits, the major towns as well as many smaller places internationally well-known or having special local significance; and also including the names of major physical features.

ABBREVIATIONS

Austral. - Australia
B.C. - British Columbia
C. - Cape
Calif. - California
Can. - Canada
chan. - channel
Dem. - Democratic
E. - East
Eng. - England
Fed. - Federal
G. - Gulf
Gt. - Great
Hd. - Head
I./Is. - Island, Islands
Mt. - Mount
Mts. - Mountains
N. - North
Nat. - National
N.Y. - New York (state)
N.Z. - New Zealand
Pen. - Peninsula
prov. - province
Pt. - Point
R. - River
reg. - region
Rep. - Republic
S. - South
Scot. - Scotland
Sd. - Sound
Str. - Strait
Terr. - Territory
U.K. - United Kingdom
W. - West

Name	Map	Grid
Luton	4	F6
Luxembourg	10	E4
L'vov	10	G3
Lyme Bay	2	C7
Lyon	10	E4
Macapa	18	E2
Macau	12	O6
Macdonnell Range	19	D3
Macgillycuddy's Reeks	7	A5
Mackenzie R.	15	E2
McKinley, Mt.	15	C2
Macquarie I.	21	C7
Madagascar	14	G7
Madang	21	C5
Madeira Is.	14	A1
Madison	16	H4
Madras	12	L7
Madrid	10	D4
Magellan, Str. of	17	D8
Maine	16	K4
Maitland	19	G10
Majorca	10	E5
Makasar Str.	11	O9
Malaga	10	D5
Malanje	14	D5
Malawi	14	F6
Malawi, L.	13	F6
Malay Peninsula	11	N8
Malaysia	12	N8
Maldives	22	N4
Mali	14	B3
Malin Hd.	7	D1
Malmö	10	F3
Malta	10	F5
Malvern Hills	2	D5
Man, Isle of	4	B3
Managua	16	J7
Manaus	18	D3
Manchester	3	D4
Manchester, Greater, co.	3	D4
Manchuria	12	P4
Mandalay	12	M6
Mangalore	12	K7
Manila	12	O7
Manitoba	16	H3
Manitoba, L.	15	G3
Manizales	18	C2
Maputo	14	F7
Mar del Plata	18	E6
Maracaibo	18	C1
Maramba	14	E6
Maree, L.	5	C3
Marianas	21	C4
Marquesas Is.	21	F5
Marrakech	14	B1
Marseille	10	E4
Marshall Is.	21	D4
Maryborough	19	G9
Maryland (Md.)	16	K5
Mask, L.	7	B3
Massachusetts (Mass.)	16	K4
Massawa	14	F3
Matapan, C.	9	G5
Matapo Hills	13	E7
Mato Grosso	17	E4
Maturin	18	D2
Mauritania	14	A3
Mauritius	22	N6
Mayo	8	B3
Mbeya	14	F5
Mbini	14	C4
Meath	8	E3
Mecca	12	F6
Medellin	18	C2
Mediterranean Sea	9	D5
Mekong, R.	11	M5
Melanesia	21	C4
Melbourne	19	F10
Melville I., N. Australia	19	D1
Melville I., N. Can	1	O8
Melilla	20	C7
Memphis	16	J5
Mendip Hills	2	D6
Merida	16	J6
Mersey, R.	1	D4
Merseyside	3	C4
Messina, Str. of	9	F5
Mexico	16	G6
Mexico, G. of	15	H6
Mexico City	16	H7
Miami	16	J6
Michigan	16	J4
Michigan, L.	15	J4
Micronesia	21	C3
Middlesbrough	3	E3
Midway Is.	21	E3
Milan	10	E4
Mildura	19	E10
Milwaukee	16	H4
Minneapolis	16	H4
Minnesota	16	H4
Minorca	10	E4
Minsk	10	G3
Mississippi, R.	15	H5
Mississippi, state	16	H5
Missouri R.	15	H4
Missouri, state	16	H5
Mitchell, Mt.	15	J5
Mizen Hd.	7	B5
Moçambique	14	G6
Moçâmedes	14	C6
Mogadishu	14	G4
Moluccas	21	C5
Mombasa	14	F5
Monadhliath Mts.	5	D3
Monaghan	8	D2
Mongolia	12	M4
Mongolia, Inner	12	O4
Monrovia	14	A4
Mont Blanc	9	E4
Montana	16	F4
Monte Bello Is.	19	A7
Monterrey	16	G6
Montevideo	18	E6
Montgomery	16	J5
Montreal	16	K4
Moorfoot Hills	6	E5
Moray Firth	5	E3
Morecambe Bay	1	C4
Morocco	14	A2
Moscow	10	H3
Motherwell	6	E5
Mourne Mts.	7	E2
Mozambique	14	F7
Mukden see Shenyang		
Mull	5	C4
Munich	10	E4
Murray, R.	19	E5
Murrumbidgee R.	19	F5
Muscat	12	H6
Musgrave Range	19	D3
Muztagh Ata	11	K5
Mwanza	14	F5
Mysore	12	K7
Nafud Desert	11	F6
Nairobi	14	F5
Nakuru	14	F5
Namibia (S.-W. Africa)	14	D7
Nanking	12	O5
Nantes	10	D4
Napier	20	C3
Naples	10	F4
Narvik	10	F2
Nashville	16	J5
Nassau	16	K6
Nasser, L.	13	F2
Natal, Brazil	18	G3
Natal, S. Africa	14	E7
Nauru	21	D5
N'Djamena	14	D3
Neagh, L.	7	E2
Nebraska	16	G4
Needles, The	2	E7
Nene, R.	2	F5
Nepal	12	L6
Ness, L.	5	D3
Netherlands	10	E3
Nevada	16	F5
New Brunswick	16	L4
New Caledonia	21	D6
New England Range	19	G4
New Forest	2	E7
New Guinea	21	C5
New Hampshire (N.H.)	16	K4
New Hebrides see Vanuatu		
New Jersey (N.J.)	16	K4
New Mexico	16	G5
New Orleans	16	J6
New Plymouth	20	B2
New S. Wales	19	F10
New York, city	16	K4
New York, state	16	K4
Newcastle, New S. Wales	19	G10
Newcastle-upon-Tyne, Eng.	3	E2
Newfoundland	16	L3
Newry	8	E2
Niagara Falls	15	K4
Niamey	14	C3
Nicaragua	16	J7
Nicaragua, L.	15	J7
Nice	10	E4
Nicobar Is.	12	M8
Niger	14	C3
Niger, R.	13	C3
Nigeria	14	C3
Nile, R.	13	F2
Nîteroi	18	F5
Norfolk, Eng.	3	G5
Norfolk, Virginia	16	K5
Norfolk Broads	1	H5
Norfolk I.	21	D6
Norrköping	10	F3
North Cape, N.Z.	20	B1
North Cape, Norway	10	G1
North Channel	7	E1
North Downs	2	F6
North Foreland	2	H6
North Island	20	B2
North Minch	5	B2
North Pole	20	D8
North Sea	9	D3
North West Highlands	5	C3
North-West Territories	16	E2
Northam	19	B10
Northamptonshire	4	E5
Northern European Plain	9	F3
Northern Ireland	8	D2
Northern Territory	19	D7
Northumberland	3	D2
Norway	10	E2
Norwegian Sea	9	D2
Norwich	4	H5
Notre Dame Mts.	15	K4
Nottingham	3	E5
Nottinghamshire	3	E4
Nouadhibou	14	A2
Nouakchott	14	A2
Nova Scotia	16	L4
Novaya Zemlya	11	H1
Novosibirsk	12	L3
Nubian Desert	13	F2
Nullarbor Plain	19	C4
Nürnberg	10	F4
Nyasa, L.	13	F6
Oakland	16	E5
Ob, R.	11	J2
Oban	6	C4
Ochil Hills	5	E4
Odense	10	E3
Odessa	10	H4
Offaly	8	D3
Ogbomosho	14	C4
Ohio	16	J4
Okhotsk, Sea of	11	R3
Oklahoma, state	16	H5
Oklahoma City	16	G5
Öland	10	F3
Olympia	16	E4
Olympus, Mt.	9	G5
Omagh	8	D2
Omaha	16	H4
Oman	12	H7
Oman, G. of	11	H6
Omsk	12	K3
Omdurman	14	F3
Onega, L.	9	H2
Ontario	16	H4
Ontario, L.	15	K4
Oporto	10	D4
Oran	14	C1
Orange, R.	13	D7
Orange Free State	14	E7
Oregon	16	E4
Orinoco, R.	17	D2
Orkney	6	C1
Osaka	12	Q5
Oslo	10	E2
Ottawa	16	K4
Ouse, R.	1	E4
Ouse, Gt. R.	2	G5
Oxford	4	E6
Oxfordshire	4	E6
Ozark Plateau	15	H5
Pacific Ocean	21	D4
Pagalu	14	C5
Paisley	6	D5
Pakistan	12	J6
Palermo	10	F5
Palk Str.	11	L7
Palliser, C.	20	C3
Palmerston North	20	B3
Pamirs	11	K5
Pampas	17	D6
Panama	16	J8
Panama, city	16	K8
Panama, G. of	17	B2
Panama, Isthmus of	15	J8
Papua New Guinea	21	C5
Paraguay	18	D5
Paramaribo	18	E2
Parana, R.	17	E6
Paris	10	E4
Patagonian Desert	17	C8
Peace R.	15	F3
Peak, The	1	E4
Pearl Harbor	21	E4
Peipus, L.	9	G3
Peking	12	O5
Peloponnesus Pen.	9	G5
Pennines	1	D3
Pennsylvania (Pa.)	16	K4
Pentland Firth	5	E2
Pentland Hills	5	E5
Penzance	4	A7
Perth, Scot.	6	E4
Perth, W. Australia	19	A10
Peru	18	C3
Philadelphia	16	K5
Philippines	12	P7
Phnom Penh	12	N7
Phoenix	16	F5
Phoenix Is.	21	E5
Pickering, Vale of	1	F3
Pierre	16	G4
Pietermaritzburg	14	F7
Pindus Mts.	9	G5
Pisa	10	E4
Pitcairn I.	21	F6
Pittsburg	16	K4
Plenty, Bay of	20	C2
Ploesti	10	G4
Plovdiv	10	G4
Plymouth	4	B7
Plynlimon	2	C5
Poland	10	F3
Polynesia	21	E6
Popocatepetl	15	G7
Port-au-Prince	16	K7
Port Augusta	19	D10
Port Elizabeth	14	E8
Port Harcourt	14	C4
Port Moresby	21	C5
Port of Spain	18	D1
Port Pirie	19	D10
Port Said	14	F1
Port Sudan	14	F2
Portland	16	E4
Portland Bill	2	D7
Pôrto Alegre	18	E5
Portsmouth	4	E7
Portugal	10	D5
Powys	4	C5
Poznań	10	F3
Prague	10	F3
Preston	3	D4
Pretoria	14	E7
Prince Edward I. (P.E.I.)	16	L4
Prince Rupert	16	D3
Pripet Marshes	9	G3
Providence	16	K4
Puebla	16	H7
Punta Arenas	18	C8
Pusan	12	P5
Pyongyang	12	P5
Pyrenees	9	D4
Qatar	12	H6
Qattara Depression	13	E2
Quantock Hills	2	C6
Quebec, city	16	K4
Quebec, prov.	16	K3
Queen Alexandra Range	20	F4
Queen Charlotte Is.	15	D3
Queen Mary Land	20	H3
Queen Maud Range	20	F3
Queensland	19	E8
Quito	18	C3
Reindeer L.	15	G3
Reykjavik	10	B2
Rhine, R.	9	E3
Rhode Island (R.I.)	16	K4
Rhodes	10	G5
Rhodesia see Zimbabwe		
Rhodope Mts.	9	G4
Rhondda Valley	2	C6
Rhone, R.	9	E4
Ribble, R.	1	D4
Richmond	16	K5
Riga	10	G3
Riga, G. of	9	G3
Rio de Janeiro	18	F5
Rio Grande	15	G6
Riyadh	12	G6
Rockhampton	19	G8
Rocky Mts.	15	D3
Romania	10	G4
Rome	10	F4
Roraima	17	D2
Rosario	18	D6
Roscommon	17	C3
Ross Dependency	20	F5
Ross Sea	20	F4
Rostov	12	G4
Rotarua	20	C2
Rotterdam	10	E3
Ruapehu, Mt.	20	C3
Rub al Khali Desert	11	G7
Rudolf, L.	13	F4
Ruwenzori	13	F4
Rwanda	14	E5
Sabah	12	O8
Sacramento	16	E5
Sahara	13	B2
Saigon	12	N7
St. Abb's Head	5	F5
St. Andrews	6	F4
St. Bees Head	1	C3
St. Davids Head	2	A6
St. Etienne	10	E4
St. George's Channel	7	F5
St. Helena	14	B6
St. John	16	L4
St. Lawrence, G. of	15	L4
St. Lawrence R.	15	L4
St. Louis	16	H5
St. Paul	16	H4
Salem	16	E4
Salford	3	D4
Salisbury, Eng	4	E6
Salisbury Plain	2	D6
Salop see Shropshire		
Salt Lake City	16	F4
Salvador	18	G4
Salween, R.	11	M6
Salzburg	10	F4
Samarkand	12	J5
Samoa	21	E5
San Cristobal	16	C2
San Diego	16	F6
San Francisco	16	E5
San Jorge, G.	17	D7
San José	16	H7
San Lucas, C.	15	F6
San Marino	10	F4
San Roque, C.	17	G3
San Salvador	16	H7
Sana	12	G7
Santa Cruz, Argentina	18	D8
Santa Cruz, Bolivia	18	D4
Santa Fé, Argentina	18	D6
Santa Fe, New Mexico	16	G5
Santarém	18	E3
Santiago	18	C6
Santos	18	F5
Sao Luis	18	F3
Sao Paulo	18	E5
Sao Tome & Principe	14	C4
Sapporo	12	R4
Saragossa	10	D4
Sarajevo	10	F4
Sarawak	12	O8
Sardinia	10	E5
Saskatchewan	16	G3
Saskatchewan R.	15	G3
Saskatoon	16	F3
Saudi Arabia	12	F6
Sayan Mts.	11	M3
Scafell Pike	1	C3
Scandinavian Pen.	9	F2
Scilly, Is. of	inset 4	A8
Scoresbysund	22	L1
Seattle	16	E4
Seine, R.	9	E4
Selsey Bill	2	F7
Senegal	14	A3
Seoul	12	P5